POODUNNIT

M

MORTIMER

PICTURE CREDITS
The publishers would like to thank the following sources for their kind permission to reproduce the pictures in this book. Key: T=top, B=bottom, L=left, R=right, C=center.

Alamy Stock Photo: /BIOSPHOTO: 30TL; /bjphotographs: 4R, 24TL; /Ulrich Doering: 12TR; /Dorling Kindersley ltd: 9B; /Thatsaphon Saengnarongrat: 16TR

Getty Images: /2ndLookGraphics/iStock: 22B; /4FR/iStock: 9T; /Arterra/UIG: 18TL; /DmitryND: 20TL; /David Fleetham/Visuals Unlimited, Inc.: 30TR; /ivstiv/iStock: 26TL; /LucynaKoch/iStock: 14TR; /photos_martYmage/iStock: 20BL; /stanley45/iStock: 10TL; /xtrekx/iStock: 26TR

Science Photo Library: /Natural History Museum, London: 24TR

Shutterstock: /AfriramPOE: 12TL; /Agnieszka Bacal: 22R; /benchart: 3T, 3BR, 4-5T, 4B, 11T, 15T, 17T, 23T, 29T; /Bildagentur Zoonar GmbH: 8BL; /Stephen Bonk: 10B; /Patrick K Campbell: 26BR; /Jim Cumming: 20BR; /FJAH: 22TL; /Svetlana Foote: 27TR; /Giedrilus: 21TR; /Dolores Harvey: 20TR; /i7do: 4C; /Jose de Jesus Churion Del: 21BR; /Sakdinon Kadchiangsaen: 28T; /Grigorita Ko: 3TL, 8TL; /Denis Kovin: 1T; /Agata Kowalczyk: 6TL; /Michael Liggett: 8TR; /Torsten Lorenz: 27BR; /Amelia Martin: 4L, 6TR; /mbrand85: 3BR, 14BR; /Al Mueller: 21BL; /Nasared: 14BL; /NaturesMomentsuk: 8BR; /PLANET EARTH: 14TL; /Dr Morley Read: 28B; /Paul Reeves Photography: 27BL; /Vaclav Sebek: 26BL; /Pises Tungittipokai: 16TL; /Vladimir Wrangel: 18TR

Every effort has been made to acknowledge correctly and contact the source and/or copyright holder of each picture and Carlton Books Limited apologises for any unintentional errors or omissions that will be corrected in future editions of this book.

Printed exclusively for Baker and Taylor

First published in Great Britain in 2019 by Carlton Books Limited.
This edition published in the United States in 2021 by
Mortimer Children's Books
An imprint of Welbeck Children's Limited,
part of the Welbeck Publishing Group
20 Mortimer Street, London W1T 3JW

Text and design copyright © 2019 Welbeck Children's Limited,
part of the Welbeck Publishing Group

ISBN: 978-1-83935-105-1

Printed in Dongguan, China
10 9 8 7 6 5 4 3 2 1

Writer: Meg Wellington
Designed and packaged by: Raspberry Books
Creative Director: Clare Baggaley
Editorial Manager: Joff Brown

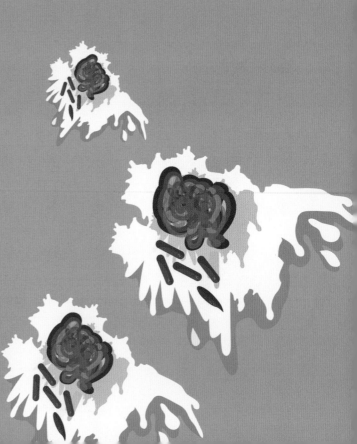

CONTENTS

IMPORTANT POOP

Every animal poops differently, and all poops hold clues about who made them. So examining poop is a great way to find out about wildlife. For many animals, pooping and peeing are a way to communicate. They are saying, "I've been here!" or "Keep away, this is my patch!"

SCAT is the name for poop found in the wild.

Some animal scat is tube-shaped.

Other animal scat comes as small round pellets.

Some poop comes in blobs or squirts.

WHAT PUTS THE SMELL IN A POOP?

Animals that eat only plants do mild-smelling poop. Meat eaters have much smellier poop.

TRACKS AND TRAILS

Wild animals leave tracks and trails along with their scat. Look out for their footprints, claw marks, and scratchings. Anyone can be an animal detective. When you know what to look for, there are clues everywhere!

WHOSE POOP?

Can you guess who made these two?

🔍 CLUES

- This animal only eats plants not other animals.
- The poop may be small, but the animal isn't!
- This animal is often hunted by cougars, wolves ... and humans.

CLUES

- This animal will eat anything it can find!
- It can howl, but it's not a wolf.
- This scavenger is sometimes found in big cities, rooting through trash.

SCAT STATS

Size: Medium
Shape: Oblong
Number: 2–6
Stinkiness: 8/10
Special features: Often spotted by the side of the road

SCAT STATS

Size: Small
Shape: Round
Number: 20–30
Stinkiness: 3/10
Special features: Sometimes found clustered together

TURN OVER to find out!

DEER POOP

Deer eat grass and leaves. They turn these into lots of little pellets that get scattered over the ground where they feed.

FACT

When deer are startled, they poop right away. No point in carrying it all around when you're trying to escape a predator!

COYOTE POOP

Coyotes are scavengers who love to eat all kinds of small, furry animals, but they will also snack on fruit when they're hungry. So coyote poop might have berries in it … or the fur and bones of small creatures.

FACT

Coyotes can run at speeds up to 40 miles per hour and jump across gaps up to 13 feet wide!

WHO AM I?

Claws visible

Triangle pattern

No claw marks

Very small

Looks like a dog's paw

Wild animals leave more than poop behind them. Whose prints are these?

MOOSE?

WOLF?

RABBIT?

BEAR?

Five toes

Long and narrow

Huge prints!

Two toes

Big claws

7

TURN OVER to find out!

RABBIT

Rabbits hop with their back feet landing in front of their front feet! That's why they have such unusual tracks. Watch out though—if the prints are very small, it might be a squirrel.

MOOSE

Moose are the heaviest members of the deer family. You can recognize them by their gigantic, palm-like antlers and their enormous noses! Moose are found in New England and Canada.

WOLF

Wolves have large, powerful jaws that can bite through deer bones with ease. They live in packs and can travel hundreds of miles in order to find and follow migrating animals. They can eat up to 20 pounds of meat in one meal!

GRIZZLY BEAR

Grizzlies are the biggest bears in North America. They can run at speeds up to 37 miles per hour, climb trees, and eat everything from insects to fish to plants. Even though they're very strong, they're shy and do not normally attack humans.

CREATURE CLUES

ANIMAL HOMES

Animals come in all sorts of different shapes and sizes, and so do their homes.

BATS

Bats don't build a home. Instead, they find a dark cave to roost in during the day. They live in big groups called colonies—there can be millions of bats all living together. The biggest bat colony in the world is in a cave in Texas. It is home to 20 million Mexican free-tailed bats.

SQUIRRELS

Squirrels build nests called dreys made from twigs, grass, and dry leaves. You can spot them more easily in the autumn and winter, when trees shed their leaves.

RABBITS

Some creatures make their homes underground. Rabbits dig networks of burrows, called warrens, with lots of tunnels and chambers. Warrens can be 10 feet deep and bigger than a tennis court.

WHERE'S THE BATHROOM?

Animal homes don't have bathrooms. Most creatures come outside to poop in the fresh air, and the poop near a hole in the ground can help you identify which animal lives in it. Bats poop right on the floor of the cave—there are enormous mounds of it, and it stinks!

Look on page 21 for information about birds' nests.

WHOSE POOP?

These two animals both live in African grasslands, but they're very different from one another, and so is their poop. Can you guess who made these two piles of poop?

CLUES

- This plant-eating animal is absolutely huge and has poop to match.
- It has a very special kind of nose.
- It's so strong that it can uproot trees!

SCAT STATS

Size: Very large
Shape: Rounded pellets
Number: 3–10
Stinkiness: 2/10
Special features: Contains lots of fiber because the animal doesn't digest all of the plant material it eats.

CLUES

- This animal is a ferocious hunter.
- It has a roar that can be heard five miles away.
- It lives in a group called a pride.

SCAT STATS

Size: Large
Shape: Chunks
Number: 2–3
Stinkiness: 5/10
Special features: Often dry and chalky. Used to mark territory, so found out in the open, not hidden away.

TURN OVER to find out!

AFRICAN ELEPHANT POOP

Elephants eat a lot of plants to keep their giant bodies going. Most of it comes out the other end of the animal—an elephant can produce up to 300 pounds of poop every day!

FACT

Elephant dung contains so much plant fibre that it can be made into paper!

AFRICAN LION POOP

Lions live on a meat-only diet. Female lions do most of the hunting, but only about one in three hunts results in a kill.

FACT

African lions are the second-largest big cat in the world and can weigh up to 500 pounds (tigers are even bigger, up to 660 pounds).

WHO AM I?

Like a human hand print

Four little toes with claws

ZEBRA?

GIRAFFE?

Can you figure out who these animal tracks belong to? They're all animals that are found in Africa.

MEERKAT?

BABOON?

Like a horse's hoof

Can measure 12 inches across

Two-hoofed foot

13

TURN OVER to find out!

GIRAFFE

Giraffes are the world's tallest land animals—they can grow up to 18 feet tall, and their necks can measure 6 feet! They have two hooves on each foot.

ZEBRA

There are different kinds of zebra, which all look like striped horses. Every zebra has a different pattern of stripes on its body, which helps them recognize one another.

MEERKATS

About the size of gray squirrels, meerkats live in burrows to keep them cool in the African sun. They hunt small animals, including deadly scorpions and millipedes.

BABOON

Baboons are large monkeys. They eat a wide variety of food—plant life including fruit, seeds, and grasses, and smaller animals, such as birds and rodents.

WHOSE POOP?

These animals both live in the desert. Their poop is dry, like their surroundings! Can you guess who produced these poops?

CLUES

- These animals are known as "ships of the desert".

- Like many desert creatures, they can go for a long time without drinking water.

- They can take people for a ride.

SCAT STATS

Size: Medium
Shape: Round
Number: Lots
Stinkiness: 1/10
Special features: Extremely dry.

CLUES

- This little reptile has a long tail and scaly body.

- It eats insects such as beetles, grasshoppers, and spiders.

- It basks in the sun to keep warm.

SCAT STATS

Size: Usually small
Shape: Oblong pellet with pointed ends
Number: 1
Stinkiness: 1/10
Special features: Dark brown with a white tip. The brown part contains bits of insect, such as legs and wings.

TURN OVER to find out!

CAMEL POOP

Camel dung is so dry that people use it as fuel for fires in the desert! The poop can also keep away mosquitos– but it might keep away your friends too.

FACT

Camels' humps are used to store fat, not water. If the hump is floppy, the camel is probably hungry. Camels can travel for 100 miles without water, and can drink 35 gallons in just 15 minutes!

LIZARD POOP

Lizards poop and pee from the same opening in their body. The brown part of their poop contains solid waste, and the white part contains liquid waste. The size of the poop depends on the size of the pooper!

FACT

Lizards are cold-blooded, which means their body temperature is the same as the environment around them. That means they usually live in warm places.

WHOSE POOP?

These two animals live in the icy Arctic in the far north of the world. Food here can be hard to find, so animals don't poop much! Can you guess who produced these piles?

CLUES

- This furry beast lives on land, but spends most of its time on the sea ice or in the water.
- Its excellent sense of smell can detect prey up to a mile away.
- Its giant, clawed paws are probably bigger than your face!

SCAT STATS

Size: Large
Shape: Dollop
Number: 1
Stinkiness: 5/10
Often jelly-like and dark brown, because the pooper eats lots of seal blubber. Sometimes contains bits of eggshell, bones, and seeds.

CLUES

- This tough, shaggy plant-eater is the height of a fully-grown man.
- It uses its hooves to dig through ice and snow to search for food.
- The male has a strong, musky smell to attract a mate.

SCAT STATS

Size: Large
Shape: Splatter
Number: 20 plus
Stinkiness: 2/10
Special features: moist and soft in summer, when food is plentiful. Dry and hard in winter, when food is scarce.

TURN OVER to find out!

POLAR BEAR POOP

Polar bears eat anything, from reindeer to seaweed and garbage—but they mainly hunt seals. Sometimes, when food is scarce, they go for months without a meal.

FACT

Polar bears swim for days on end in search of food. Their huge paws help them paddle for long distances, and they regularly swim more than 30 miles.

MUSK OX POOP

Musk oxen look like huge, hairy cattle, but are related to sheep and goats. They have two coats to keep them warm in winter—a shaggy outer coat and a short undercoat that drops out in the summer.

FACT

Musk oxen have four chambers in their stomach. This helps them digest the tough grasses, lichens, roots, and mosses they eat and get every bit of goodness out of them when food is scarce.

WHO AM I?

Like a dog's prints

Two bigger and two smaller prints

ARCTIC FOX?

ARCTIC HARE?

Can you figure out who these animal tracks belong to? They're all animals that are found in the Arctic.

SNOWY OWL?

HARP SEAL?

Three thin toes

Marks either side of a "drag" print

19

TURN OVER to find out!

ARCTIC FOX

Even the soles of the Arctic fox's feet are furry to keep it warm in the snow. It has a bushy tail that helps it balance and also helps keep it warm.

HARP SEAL

These seals spend most of their time in the Arctic and North Atlantic oceans, where they catch fish and crabs to eat. They can spend 15 minutes underwater without coming up for air.

ARCTIC HARE

Like some other Arctic animals, including Arctic foxes, Arctic hares grow a white winter coat to help them blend in with the snow. In summer, their coats turn brown as the snow disappears.

SNOWY OWL

The snowy owl's sharp claws help grab its prey as it swoops silently in for the kill. Like many birds, owls bring up pellets of the food they can't digest, including bones and fur.

CREATURE CLUES

BIRDS' NESTS

You can spot birds' nests in all sorts of places—in trees and bushes, on ledges, and underground. But remember, never disturb a nest, wherever it is.

BALD EAGLES

Bald eagles build giant platforms of sticks in treetops to keep their chicks safe. The nest can be up to 120 feet above ground, 20 feet deep, and weigh as much as a small car.

PUFFINS AND BURROWING OWLS

Other birds nest on or under the ground. Puffins dig a long tunnel into an earth bank. Burrowing owls simply take over abandoned burrows and avoid the hard work.

SHALLOW DIP

A shallow dip on the ground is all a plover needs to keep its eggs safe. The spotty eggshells blend with the stones and grass and are very hard to spot.

BAGS OF POOP

Baby birds poop a lot, so parents need to keep the nest clean. Newly hatched chicks produce little bags of poop called fecal sacs, which the parents swallow! Bigger chicks shuffle to the edge of the nest and poop over the side.

LOOK OUT!

Bird poop is a mixture of pee and poop. The acid in the pee turns some of the mixture white. If you see lots of white splatter spots on the ground, look out for a nest nearby.

WHOSE POOP?

The Amazon rain forest in South America is home to thousands of different kinds of creatures, and every single one of them poops! Can you guess the identity of these two Amazonian poopers?

CLUES

- This brightly colored bird squawks very loudly.

- It is very clever—some can mimic human speech.

- It has a powerful beak for cracking open nuts, seeds, and fruit.

SCAT STATS

Size: Small
Shape: Splatter
Number: Many
Stinkiness: 1/10
Special features: greenish-white. A mix of pee and poop together, so it's part solid, part liquid. Can be delivered in flight!

CLUES

- This furry creature spends most of its time hanging around in trees.

- It moves so little that green algae grows on its fur!

- Once a week it comes down to the ground to poop.

SCAT STATS

Size: Medium to large
Shape: Fat banana
Number: One (per week!)
Stinkiness: 3/10
Special features: color of a rotten banana.

TURN OVER to find out!

MACAW POOP

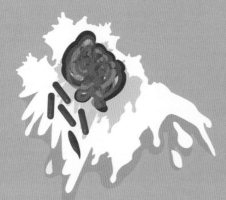

Macaws live in noisy flocks of up to 30 members. They eat seeds, fruit, nuts, and insects, but sometimes they snack on soil to settle their tummy after lots of fruit.

FACT

Like all birds, a macaw's digestive system doesn't produce gases, so it never farts.

SLOTH POOP

Sloths often get constipated, so they do a little "poop dance" to get things moving. The poop can weigh as much as one-third of the creature's body weight because it doesn't poop very often.

FACT

Sloths spend up to 80 percent of their time asleep to save energy. On land they crawl along at just three feet per minute, but they are great swimmers.

WHO AM I?

TURN OVER to find out!

Lots of tiny footprints on each side

Wavy lines

JAGUAR?

CAIMAN?

Can you figure out who these animal tracks belong to? They're all creatures that live in the Amazon rain forest.

GREEN ANACONDA?

TARANTULA?

Five toes on front foot

Four oval toe pads

Wide foot pad

Four webbed toes on back foot

25

JAGUAR

The word "jaguar" comes from a Native American word that means "he who kills with one leap." Jaguars hunt alone, sneaking up and pouncing on prey. One bite of their powerful jaws is enough to pierce a skull or crack bone.

TARANTULA

Although its bite is painful, the tarantula is not dangerous to humans—the venom is weaker than a bee sting. As it grows, a tarantula sheds its skin and replaces some body parts. It can even regrow a leg if it loses one.

CAIMAN

This scaly reptile is well suited to life in tropical rivers, lakes, swamps, and mangroves. Webbed back feet and a long, flat tail help it power through the water at speeds of 30 miles per hour in search of prey.

GREEN ANACONDA

This snake is found in tropical areas of South America. At 17 feet long, it's not quite the longest snake it the world, but it does win the prize for being the heaviest. Its only predator is the jaguar.

CREATURE CLUES

FUR AND FEATHERS

If you look very carefully on the ground and in the bushes, you can find lots more clues about which animals have been around.

Birds lose feathers as they take flight. The colors and patterns on the feathers help you figure out which kind of bird it came from.

This feather came from a male pileated woodpecker.

Mammals leave tufts of fur on fences and branches as they pass by. The color, length, and feel of the fur give clues to identify the owner.

SKIN SHEDDING

Animals without fur leave clues behind, too. Lizards and snakes shed their skins as they grow—you might be lucky enough to spot a piece.

WHAT CAN YOU SPOT?

If you look closely, you might even spot tufts of fur, feathers, or bones in poop, left over from an animal's last meal.

WHOSE POOP?

Even ocean creatures need to poop—though the evidence can be tricky to spot! Can you figure out who made these surprising poops?

CLUES

- This enormous creature lives in the ocean, but it is a mammal.

- It breathes air through a blow hole on its head.

- It communicates with others of its kind by singing.

SCAT STATS

Size: Enormous!
Shape: Cloud of slurry and chunks
Number: Many chunks
Stinkiness: 4/10
Special features: Smells fishy and floats to the surface. Color depends on the food eaten. A meal of krill (tiny shrimp-like creatures), for example, turns it bright orange.

CLUES

- This fish shares its name with a brightly colored tropical bird.

- It dines on algae found in coral.

- It has a tough beak to crunch coral.

SCAT STATS

Size: TIny
Shape: Lots of grains
Number: Impossible to count
Stinkiness: 0/10
Special features: No smell—it's just grains of sand, made from crunched up coral that passes through the fish.

29

TURN OVER to find out!

WHALE **POOP**

Different kinds of whale live in the oceans all over our planet. Some eat tiny creatures called plankton and krill. Others dine on fish, crabs, and bigger sea creatures. Their poop provides important nutrients for ocean life.

FACT

The blue whale is the largest animal ever to live on Earth. It can eat 40 million krill in one day.

PARROT FISH **POOP**

These surprising tropical fish live on coral reefs around the world. As well as pooping sand, they make their own sleeping bag out of mucus to protect themselves from hungry predators at night.

FACT

Parrot fish can change from male to female and back again all through their life.

AROUND THE WORLD
POOP QUIZ

1

Which of these creatures makes the largest poop?

a. Green anaconda
b. Elephant
c. Giraffe

2

Which animal only poops once a week?

a. Jaguar
b. Sloth
c. Polar Bear

3

Which animal's poop is used to make paper?

a. Musk ox
b. Deer
c. Elephant

4

Which animal poops sand?

a. Caiman
b. Parrot fish
c. Whale

5

Which animal's poop can be used as fuel for a fire?

a. Polar bear
b. Camel
c. Coyote

6

Which one of these animals brings up pellets of fur and bone, as well as pooping?

a. Owl
b. Tarantula
c. Caiman

7

Which of these animals never farts?

a. Lion
b. Musk ox
c. Macaw

8

Which animal poops when it is startled?

a. Deer
b. Coyote
c. Sloth

9

Which baby animals produce fecal sacs?

a. Chicks
b. Coyote pups
c. Lion cubs

10

Which creature poops and pees from the same body opening?

a. Arctic fox
b. Lizard
c. Deer